W9-BFP-344

HOW DO BIG SHIPS FLOAT?

BY ISAAC ASIMOV AND ELIZABETH KAPLAN

Gareth Stevens Publishing
MILWAUKEE

For a free color catalog describing Gareth Stevens' list of high-quality books, call 1-800-542-2595 (USA) or 1-800-461-9120 (Canada). Gareth Stevens' Fax: (414) 225-0377.

Library of Congress Cataloging-in-Publication Data

Asimov, Isaac.
How do big ships float? / by Isaac Asimov and Elizabeth Kaplan.
p. cm. — (Ask Isaac Asimov)
Includes bibliographical references and index.
Summary: Briefly describes several kinds of ships and the forces that cause them to float or sink.
ISBN 0-8368-0802-9
1. Ships— Juvenile literature. [1. Ships.] I. Kaplan, Elizabeth, 1956-. II. Title. III. Series: Asimov, Isaac. Ask Isaac Asimov.
VM150.A85 1993
623.4—dc20 92-32552

Edited, designed, and produced by
Gareth Stevens Publishing
1555 North RiverCenter Drive, Suite 201
Milwaukee, Wisconsin 53212, USA

Picture Credits
pp. 2-3, © Kirk Schlea/Picture Perfect USA; pp. 4-5, © J. E. Stevenson/Robert Harding Picture Library; pp. 6-7, © Bernard Régent/Hutchison Library; pp. 8-9, © Dick Wade/Picture Perfect USA; pp. 10-11, © Kirk Schlea/Picture Perfect USA; pp. 12-13, Tom Redman, 1992; pp. 14-15, © Ken Novak, 1992; pp. 16-17, © Fritz Prenzel/Bruce Coleman Limited; p. 17 (inset), © Mary Evans Picture Library; pp. 18-19, Courtesy of CSX Corporation; pp. 20-21, © Kirk Schlea/Picture Perfect USA; pp. 22-23, © Dr. Eckart Pott/Bruce Coleman Limited; p. 24, © Dr. Eckart Pott/Bruce Coleman Limited

Cover photograph, © B. D. Drader/Hutchison Library: The cruise liner *Oriana* is docked at Prince's Wharf in the Hauraki Gulf, in Auckland, New Zealand.

The book designer wishes to thank Jim and Ginger Montella from Blue Ribbon Pets, Inc., Milwaukee, Wisconsin, and the models for their cooperation.

Series editor: Valerie Weber
Editors: Barbara J. Behm and Patricia Lantier-Sampon
Series designer: Sabine Beaupré
Book designer: Kristi Ludwig
Picture researcher: Diane Laska

Printed in the United States of America

3 4 5 6 7 8 9 98

Contents

Words that appear in the glossary are printed in **boldface** type the first time they occur in the text.

Modern-Day Wonders

Pick up your telephone. You can have a conversation with someone halfway around the world. Turn on your VCR, and you can watch a TV program that aired last night after you went to bed. These are only a few of the many wonders of **technology**.

Big ships are another amazing scientific achievement. Some ships today are as large as a small town. How do big ships float? Let's find out.

CUNARD

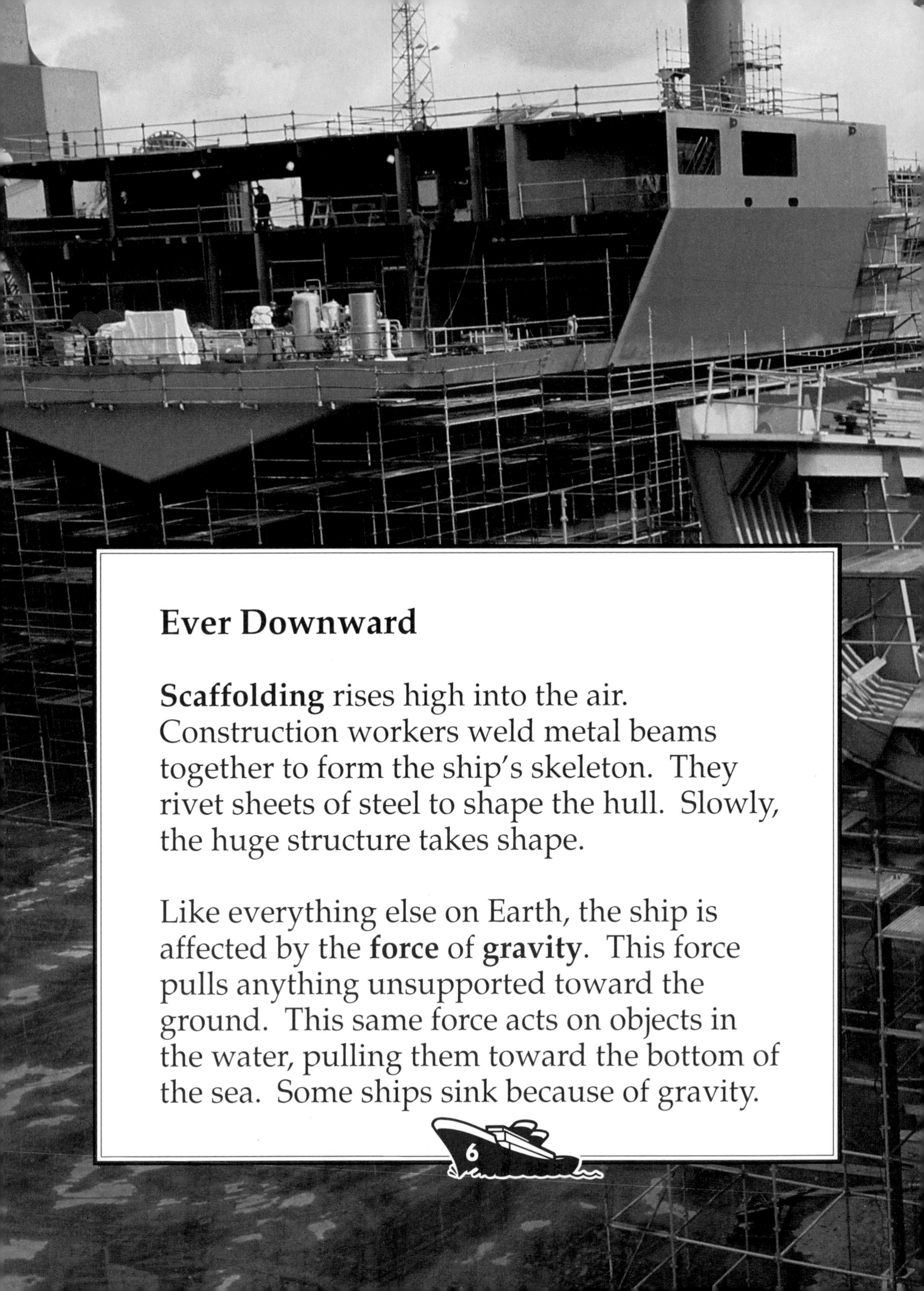

Ever Downward

Scaffolding rises high into the air. Construction workers weld metal beams together to form the ship's skeleton. They rivet sheets of steel to shape the hull. Slowly, the huge structure takes shape.

Like everything else on Earth, the ship is affected by the **force** of **gravity**. This force pulls anything unsupported toward the ground. This same force acts on objects in the water, pulling them toward the bottom of the sea. Some ships sink because of gravity.

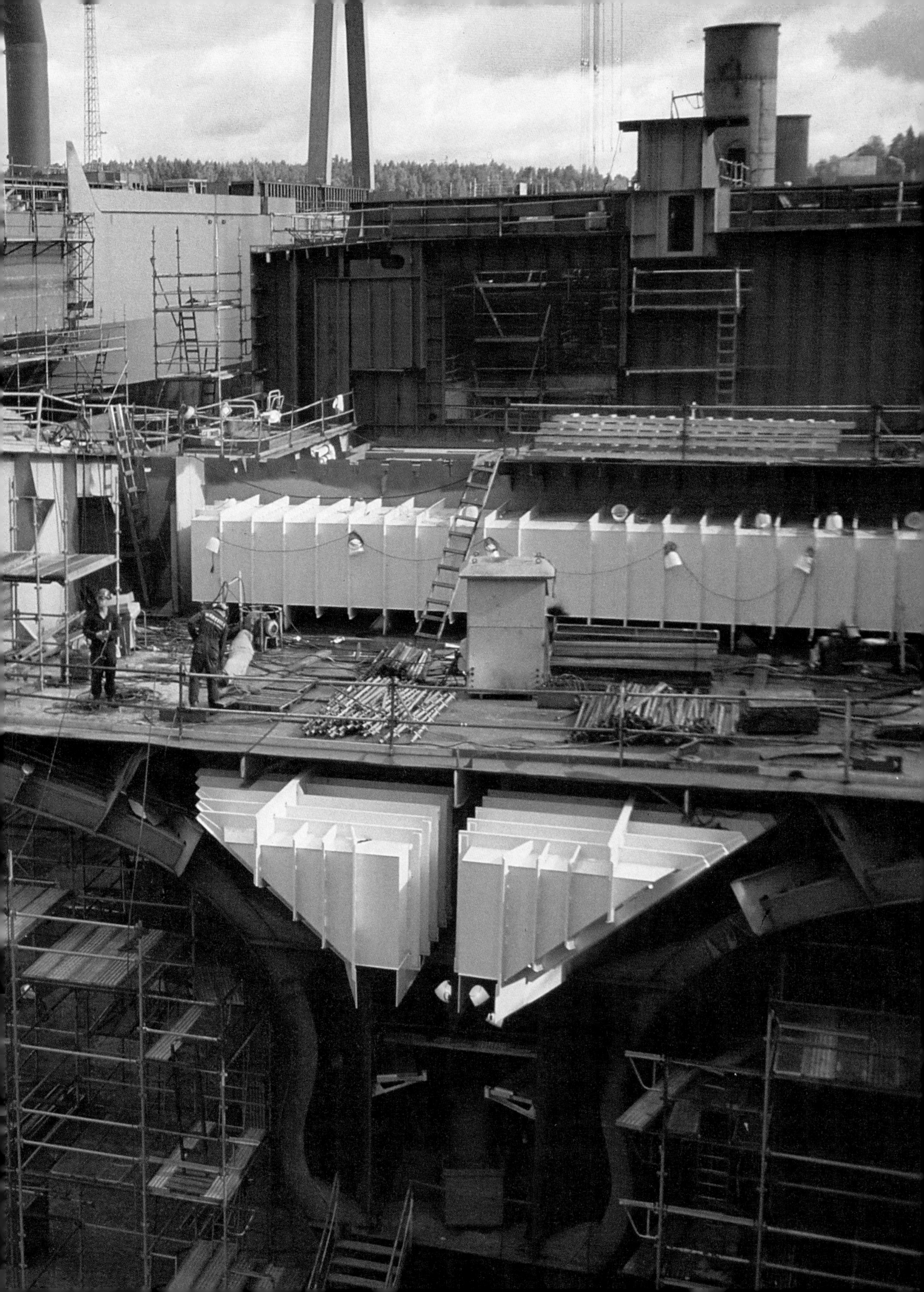

The Buoyant Force

It is a beautiful day, and you decide to go swimming. Sitting in an inner tube, you relax in the water. The river's gentle current pulls you along. With the aid of the inner

tube, you float effortlessly on the water. Water pushes up on anything placed in it. The upward push of the water is called the **buoyant force**. When the buoyant force is strong enough to overcome the force of gravity on an object, the object floats.

Sink or Float

Sadly you watch as your colorful balloon rises toward the clouds. If you let the string go, the balloon escapes into the air. The balloon floats up because it is full of helium, a gas that is lighter than air. Objects float in water for the same reason: they are lighter than water.

But it's not as simple as it sounds. A rolled-up sheet of steel sinks. But when the same steel is shaped into the hull of a ship, it floats.

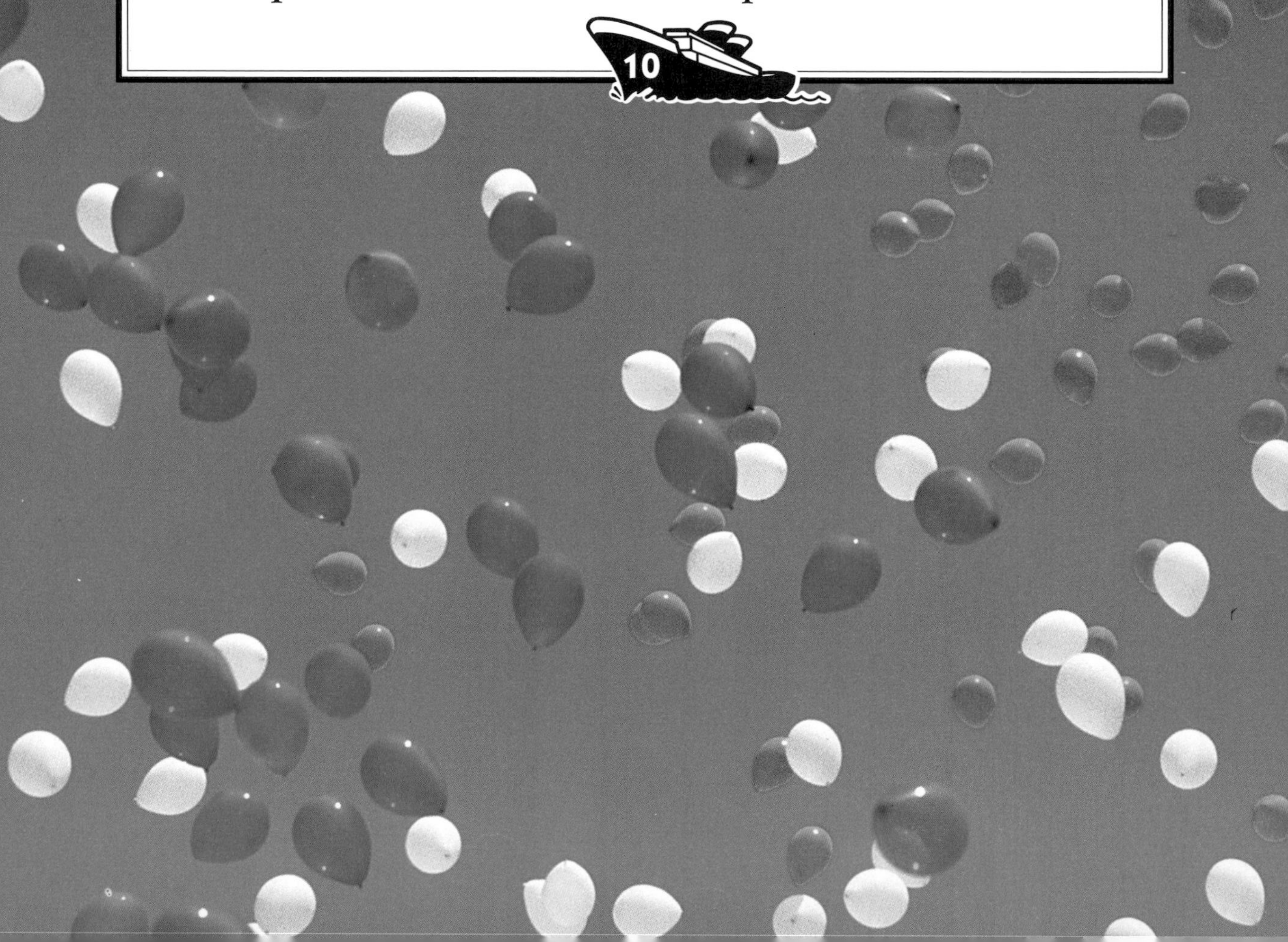

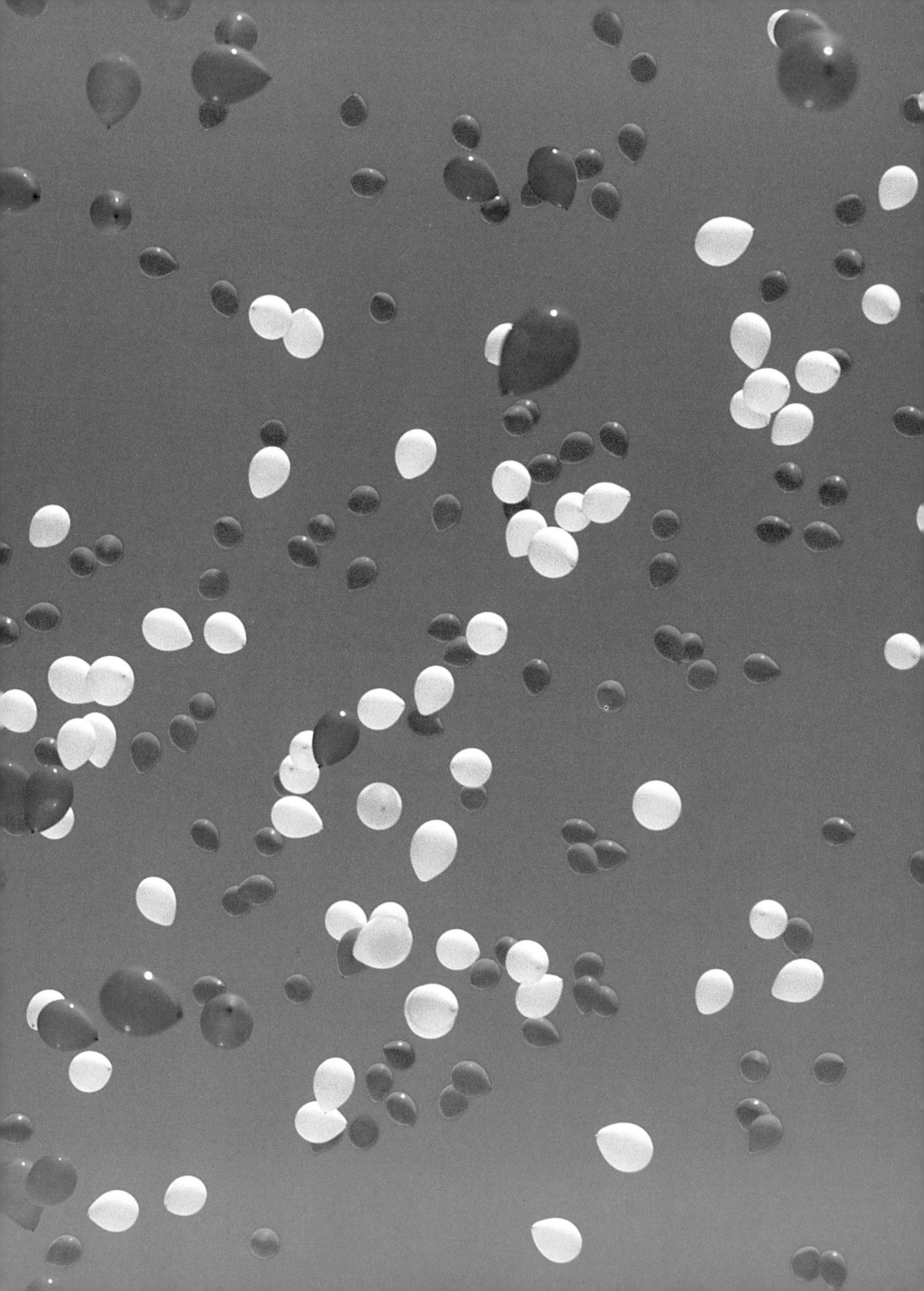

Density's the Key

An object's **volume** — the amount of space it takes up — combined with its **weight** determines whether it will sink or float. The ship's **hull**, including the air it encloses, takes up more space than the roll of steel. This means the weight of the steel is spread out over a larger volume. In other words, the ship's **density** is less than the density of the roll of steel. In fact, the ship is less dense than water. Anything less dense than water floats. Anything denser sinks.

Prove It Yourself!

Shape some clay into a ball and place it in water. Does it float? Now, shape the clay into a hollow boat. Place your boat in the water. The weight of the clay is spread out over a larger area of water. Its density is less than that of water, so your boat will float. But if your boat has a hole in it, it will take on water. This will add too much weight, and the boat will sink.

Queen Elizabeth 2
LADY WOODWARD
SYDNEY

Luxury Liners

One of the world's most famous ships is at the bottom of the sea. The *Titanic* sank on her first voyage in 1912 after hitting an iceberg. This huge luxury liner has been found on the floor of the Atlantic Ocean. Many of its ornate decorations still remain.

The *Queen Elizabeth 2* is a luxury liner whose fate has been far luckier. Her passengers enjoy a swimming pool, theater, nightclubs, and a shopping mall on cruises across the Atlantic Ocean.

SL
SEA-LAND DEVELOPER
APL

The Super Ships: Supertankers

The *Queen Elizabeth 2* is small when compared to a supertanker. The luxury liner is 963 feet (294 m) long and can hold 60,000 tons. A supertanker can carry almost ten times as much. Its sole cargo is oil.

Supertankers are the world's largest ships. They are so large that they can dock at only a few ports. Usually, supertankers are unloaded far from shore by using underwater pipes or by transferring their oil to smaller ships.

Exploring the Ocean Floor

Some ships are useful not because they float, but because they sink. **Submarines** take in water through special chambers, allowing them to sink. They can dive down to the ocean floor and cruise along.

To rise back to the surface, the submarine forces out the water it contains. **Compressed** air is pumped into the chambers, making the sub less dense than the water. The ship becomes buoyant and rises to the surface.

From Ripples to Waves

From delicate ripples on a starlit pond to thundering waves on stormy seas, water fascinates us in all its forms. Thanks to our understanding of what makes things float, we have built ships of all kinds to safely enjoy and explore the world's lakes, oceans, and waterways.

More Books to Read

Freighters: Cargo Ships and the People Who Work Them by George Ancona (Crowell)
The Ship in the Field by Henny and Luciano Bufchini (Scroll Press)
Ships by N. F. Barrett (Franklin Watts)
Ships and Seaports by Katherine Carter (Childrens Press)
Submarines by C. J. Norman (Franklin Watts)

Places to Write

Here are some places you can write for more information about ships, big and small. Be sure to tell them exactly what you want to know. Give them your full name and address so they can write back to you.

Mystic Seaport
50 Greenmanville Avenue
Mystic, Connecticut 06355

Titanic Historical Society
P.O. Box 51053
Indian Orchard, Massachusetts 01151

Mariners' Museum
100 Museum Drive
Newport News, Virginia 23606

Nova Scotia Museum
Department of Maritime History
1747 Summer Street
Halifax, Nova Scotia B3H 3A6

Glossary

buoyant force (BOY-ant FORS): the force that results from water pushing up on an object. If the buoyant force is strong enough to counteract gravity, the object floats.

compressed (cuhm-PREHST): forced to occupy a smaller space than normal.

density (DEHN-suh-tee): the weight of an object divided by its volume.

force: a push or pull that changes an object's speed or the direction in which it is moving.

gravity (GRAV-uh-tee): the force that pulls everything toward the center of the Earth.

hull: the body of a ship, not including the masts, sails, rigging, deck, or buildings on the deck.

scaffolding: a temporary platform for workers to stand or sit on when working above the floor or ground.

submarine (suhb-muh-REEN): a ship that can cruise under water.

technology (tehk-NAH-luh-jee): the use of scientific principles to produce things that are useful to people.

volume (VAHL-yoom): the amount of space an object takes up.

weight (WAYT): the measure of how heavy an object is.

Index